REVOLVER

KUHL HOUSE POETS
EDITED BY
MARK LEVINE AND BEN DOLLER

POEMS BY ROBYN SCHIFF

Revolver

UNIVERSITY OF IOWA PRESS · IOWA CITY

University of Iowa Press, Iowa City 52242
Copyright © 2008 by Robyn Schiff
www.uiowapress.org
Printed in the United States of America

Design by Kristina Kachele Design, llc

The University of Iowa Press is a member of Green Press Initiative and is committed to preserving natural resources.

Printed on acid-free paper

Library of Congress Cataloging-in-Publication Data
Schiff, Robyn.
Revolver: poems / by Robyn Schiff.
p.   cm.—(Kuhl House Poets)
ISBN-13: 978-1-58729-695-6 (pbk.)
ISBN-10: 1-58729-695-0 (pbk.)
I. Title.
PS3619.C365R48 2008
811'.6—dc22   2008009633

08 09 10 11 12 P 5 4 3 2 1

These are still for Nick.

Contents

Acknowledgments

I offer my sincere gratitude to the editors of the following journals, where some of these poems first appeared: *Canary, Chicago Review, Columbia Poetry Review, Court Green, Denver Quarterly, jubilat, Kiosk, MAKE, Octopus, Poetry Daily, A Public Space*, and *Seattle Review*. Additionally, some of this work has been represented in anthologies, and I am grateful to the editors of these publications as well: *The City Visible: Chicago Poetry for the New Century* (Cracked Slab Books) and *Women Poets on Mentorship: Efforts and Affections* (University of Iowa Press).

Thank you for your insights and the inspiration of your work: Erica Bernheim, Eula Biss, Averill Curdy, Michael Dumanis, Josh Edwards, Andrew Feld, Cate Marvin, David Trinidad, Emily Wilson, Leila Wilson, and Tim Wood. I am grateful for the support of my mother and my father, and my sister, Stacy Schiff. These poems have benefited tremendously from the editorial vision of Mark Levine, as well as that of Suzanne Buffam and Srikanth Reddy, and Pimone Triplett; with deep gratitude to each of you.

Thank you, Holly Carver and the University of Iowa Press.

REVOLVER

Colt Rapid Fire Revolver

The wedding cake of Elizabeth Hart (Colt since
noon) was trimmed with sugar pistols
with revolving sweet-tooth chambers with gears
that rotate one position over like a
dancer down a dance line
prompted by an aisle that parts in music
to switch partners while a

fly drawn to the sugar places a stringy foot
on the trigger. Dysentery.
There must be a gallery with bull's-eyes
blown through sugar faces spun on the same scale
and a wife at a sewing
bee bridging a scarf like a ray of house-
fly regurgitation

between her sticky knitting needles who admits
that when her husband said he'd be
at the gallery she assumed he meant
to see pictures she was too innocent to
see. She imagined him hat
in hand leaning toward a battle scene and
deep in the grainy wound

in the painting's newly dead, indeed a bullet
too deep to see gleams beyond the
vanishing point in both his vision as
he aims and fires in target practice, and hers,
as she conjures past a line
she would never cross on foot following
the caravan of her

thinking in tedious steps over internal
prairie until it overcomes
the body of her youngest catching
a fly off an ox's tail while the
oxen are moving and yet
onward the party continues until
the provisions of her

fantasy wear thin. Though this is manifest in
sugar, it still disturbs me when
the Donner Party built to scale with the
Patented Colt Revolvers trimming this cake
melt their weakest into a
desperate sap. Though the world's first sugar
bowl was passed from guest to

guest to show the wealth of Elizabeth's court when
an ounce of sugar traded for
a calf, it's worth more than that. You demur
to mourn lives lost on the frontier raised in scale
and substance to people the
West the Patented Colt Revolvers that
trim a cake were cast to

defend, but I say the bull's-eyes marksmen see mapped
upon the apples poised on the
heads of all things are cut on a lathe whose
smallest revolution of thought is in sync
with that which shapes the metal
of the revolving chamber whose circular
machinations synchronize

with the rings a fly circling the bullet wound
makes in air. Focus my gaze; I
see like a fly whose vision is more like
several interlocking rings left by a tea-
cup on a book but the cake
was six feet high and how could I resist
pistols winding tier up-

on tier up the icing reverberating in
decoration the prudence of
a revolver's placement in the holsters
of a row of guards under whose raised arms that
beam a private arbor the
bride and bridegroom enter their union. Re-
petition of pistols

map a rebus of progress marching since the first
firearms to devise a weapon
that can repeat fire without reloading.
Behold the rapid fire pistol inspired
by Colt's meditations on
the wheel of the ship steering him toward
India spinning and

locking in position like the machinations
of fortune pacing through the in-
finite face of its clock in such baby
steps that I shall reign I reign I reigned adjust
the powers of judgment en-
trusted to calibrate them. Leaning in
to see the gears, like the

wick of one candle used to light the next all along
a dark corridor, leaning in
and replicating, is not unlike the
vision the sugar wife had of her sugar
husband leaning in to see
the detail of a battle painting, and
stirred by the fire there,
enlisting.

de la Rue's Envelope Machine ·

With output of twenty-seven hundred
envelopes an hour
where prior but
three thousand were made a day, cry
when you consider the empty envelopes piled
on each of our desks it is our
responsibility to load and

send, inserting therein a folded note
in an action that
reverses the
process of the envelope stock
itself having once been inserted flat into
the machine bed and exiting
folded in the automation of

the same paper-folding mystery of
which it is said some
performers snap
jerking, flapping birds from sheets of
paper in such a glare of footlights, that folding
this quickly along pre-laid creases

appears to be the instantaneous
transformation of
matter. A toy,
an ornament, one thousand cranes
folded in a plea for longevity by she
afflicted with the "atom bomb
disease" who, in taking the napkin

from her lap to fold beside her plate, and
later in folding
the bed sheets back,
knows her hands fold for good. Friend, don't
unbend, to see what's written, even one wing of
the paper crane the king's master
folder made of the document you're

transporting. Your inability to
fold it back will be
cited by the
master unfolder at your brief
treason hearing. His sword is origami, as
swords are. Its hammered folds have the
audacity never to unfold—

an envelope with no opening that
holds your life—

    inside, along the pre-laid crease, my last
        words laid beside my first, or lying? I
        make mistakes a lot, it holds me back I
    think, or thought, the moments pass by so fast

    they make a liar of me. I once thought glass
        orchids made the perfect gift as I'm
        too slow to see a real one before it dies
    by my own hand, but I think instead I'll ask

    you for a tissue-paper rose fanned
    around a central pipe-cleaner stem, petals

lightweight as the man-
ifold paper
once used to make carbon copies,
whose petals, unlike an origami fortune
wheel which opens to reveal yes
no yes no, reveal nothing. Isn't

the parlor game Consequences, based on
the concealment of
the details of
a continuing saga from
the eyes of its several authors who each fold
over what she's written before
passing it on, foiled if no one

unfolds it, finally? like a dollar in
a billfold loses
its charm unless
exchanged for something or, through the
Art of U.S. Dollar Bill Folding, becomes an
object of papery desire:
paper diamond ring, paper bow tie,

pair of paper cowboy chaps standing with-
out torso in the
bowed posture of
the lower half of John Wayne o-
ver a paper desert, two dollar empire on
my dresser. The escape artist
Houdini, who wrote a book on pa-

per magic, knew it was something akin
to the intricate
security
flourishes, the electric fence
on the face of the dollar, that kept the signs he
sent his wife from reaching her long
after his death. Secure transactions.

A silence. An atmosphere envelopes
us and furthermore,
automating
the folding of envelopes in
which to seal the embossed lace letter papers, cards
for wedding and mourning, and at-
home cards the stationer also makes

won't help me distinguish myself among
many who use this
ATM, this
American Express Travelers
Cheque which I shall endorse by presenting my New
York State driver license instead
of using the currency abroad

(I neither drive nor live in New York State),
all fine printed by
De La Rue whose
business "is entrusted to se-
cure transactions world wide," and just last May chartered
twenty-seven gorgeous Boeing
747s to deliv-

er currency to Iraq. Stand outside
the fence, Nick. What I
wouldn't give to
deliver this myself. Stand out-
side the fence. I pass this through the silence of the
cranes to you.

House of Schiaparelli

Of the cocktail dress with painted lobster—
tail fanning like a red codpiece from which
the red lobster
writhes on the bias down the thigh of she who cuts
the buffet line—do not say it
swirls like the floor of a private
ocean across which you would like to live

with one long book, water lapping as she
walks like white waves carving coves in moonrock
through which as-yet
undiscovered fish flash mating radar back and
forth depths glowing as if lit by
a string of pearls; this lobster is
cooked. It banged on the lobster pot boiling

alive. Consider how the organza
skirt organizes candlelight it moves
through with the same
haze a porcelain plate makes passing boy-girl-boy-girl-
boy down one side of a dinner
table and back, the translucent
surface it took European potters

centuries to steal from China like a
fading complexion through which lines of blue
blood can almost
be seen in transit from a distance, like canals
on Mars, persistent, pulsing with
commerce lost to us like Roman
baths in England, smelling like rotten eggs

when divers leave life forms that breathe iron
in temperatures that melt lead on the ship's
deck in vials
and return to sea vents so deeply wrought that a
Pacific diver will nearly
meet an Atlantic diver in
the core of the earth like one's right and left

hands almost touching through separate pockets
behind a pleat. Manufacture of the
inessential
halted, when a button factory no longer
presses mother-of-pearl buttons
from oyster shells, a jacket made
to stay closed with dog chain once linking dogs

to their posts hangs in the closet while loose
dogs roam. Released from guard duty, dogs crouch
beside each of
us so quickly, perhaps the dog was inside all
along, but that, like the child's doll
in which the wolf and Riding Hood
both abide, a flip of the long white skirt

revealing each with the other's torso
facing back where legs should be suggests how
debilitat-
ing inner life—lying in bed all day, pillows
on both ends, shared skirt propped like a
surgical screen between them, they
listen for a faraway "stay" as if

spoken from a second moon, dull daylight
moon without phases that neither waxes
nor wanes but just
ruminates, stirring cursed bayers to circle the
rug again, dream another dream
in which objects of real life don't
assume new shades but stand for themselves on

the mantelpiece of sleep. But since Mrs.
Wallis Simpson, who says she never wants
to be Queen, wore
the lobster dress in public to press the British
press to find her whimsical as
a lobster at a fundraiser
despite having walked away with their King,

please allow me to show you how lobster
and werewolf share the same breath when I say
"hello" into
the lobster telephone receiver inspired by
the same Salvador Dalí sketch,
given that Cockney rhyming slang
for telephone is dog and bone and it's

just a quick dash up the back apples from
there to see moonlight on the moor transform
the encoded
beast. I'm halfway through *The Hound of the Baskervilles*
and hope the hound is real. Choose your
dress well, Mrs. Simpson, like whom
I do not want to be Queen, you might wear

it into exile and still be in it
passing secrets over the phone to the
Ambassador
of Germany. Dalí's lobster phone, I'm thinking.
What kind of world is this? Between
whispers, resting the lobster hand-
set on your shoulder while you stir your tea

two lobsters unbearably proximate
cancel you out, Mrs. Wallis Simpson.
Reports of were-
wolves attacking guard dogs test what gauge steel links the
food chain. How it doubles back on
itself. Hitler's pack of trained Were-
wolves, an army within an army track

their own tracks. In the eyes of youth gleams the
independence of beasts, Hitler said of
his youngest Were-
wolves. Trained with a little patience, he meant. Transformed
by the moon into the moon's wolf,
a man who mauled his wife by night
was discovered with the red thread of her

cloak in his teeth. It doesn't matter if
you believe in werewolves or not if they're
real, like jewels, of
which the opposite is true. I'm embarrassed to
admit it, but it's taken a
few lonely weeks to end this poem
and in the meantime I finished *The Hound*

of the Baskervilles, which indeed was real,
with a little stagecraft. Footsteps of its
giant breed set
beside those of a lapdog displayed at Scotland
Yard in 1951 a-
lert us to the unwieldiness
of categories. How inclusive!

Do I not understand what Dalí meant
calling Hitler his surrealist brother?
In addition
to the King and a car salesman, Wallis Simpson
also loved the Woolworth heir; see
her choosing an industrial
Woolworth diadem at the counter, Queen
of the cooked world.

Singer Sewing Machine

His costume, his body stocking,
dulls him like dark circles cast all the way down his body
the morning after being awake forever,
the dancer dancing death collecting the other cast members, recollections
from the other side
—steps were taken, and we were all there—
on the couch of the late-night talk show   in his warm hand   from the plastic
maraca of his bottle of Tylenol PM, tiny suicide rattle, baby step, do it again, louder,
from the glass on the bedside table   louder, from the automatic icemaker
dumping its dollop-shaped ice again   a routine forming   from the cover of the
library book falling against the title page   from the thump of the newspaper at
the front door, it must be the end of the world, it must be the end of the hook   it
must be the end of the war   drawn by a force a force a force   drawn into the
overcast sky
of his count
his opening bag,
gun smoke, a token death,
a saying-of-a-thing-once step,
you-have-a-very-important-statement-
to-make step, you-say-it-once-clearly step,
you-take-steps step, are taken by the steps
of the dancer up the theater steps,
in stages of transport and transcendence,
in five stages of death *The Green Table*
draws a different dancer from the dance
in each of eight danced scenes: The Gentlemen
in Black, The Dance of Death and Farewells,
The Battle, The Refugee, The Partisan,
The Brothel, The Aftermath, The Gentlemen
in Black.
Imagine both the pistol and the pocket
in regard to the hand; imagine the boot

and the pedal; the not-bad-do-it-again;
the darkness of the audience; the curb and the head; the stand; and when the taking
takes, why should I tell you what to do with the body? When the plume shakes I see
the profiteer take several steps past; when I say step, I mean stamp. No, this will not
leave a mark. The secret is in the program: read the names: the dancers dance two
roles; but I saw the whole dance and never noticed any of them coming back.

※ ※

Back them into the dance, I say, the roles reverse the dancers' names. Does the
program list the secrets of the audience? Mark this: stamping her foot in darkness,
Daisy Fellowes, heiress to the Singer Sewing Machine fortune in a new dress printed
with hundreds of poodles on leash each in a leather collar stamped inside with its
owner's name: DF: I see this, but you don't. Each memory must compensate
for its own dream, I say,
stepping past you into the eye of the seated dog,
many steps past its mistress' lax hand in the loop
of the leash
from which all thing are drawn
into profit. I have a pen with a plume
with which I sign off on the body.
You squirm. I stand in my head.
You stop at the curb, I drive on.
The audience in darkness
shifts in a community, as each harnessed
dog in hitch is but a pedal in the sled's speed,
each a boot in the march. When the hand
drops the leash and moves toward the pocket
there is only one pistol, gentlemen, one
black dream to set things going and I
don't know if this is it
or its aftermath.

At the brothel partisan
and refugee share the same hand towel.
Battle of Farewells   Battle of Pause   Death is a rhythm dogs see in the dance
of light on black ice   from the Gentlemen of Scene Change   dance of properties,
and dancer of   The table is green and they were all seated there in the name of
diplomacy, death in stages   and Daisy in transcendent dress with poodles leashed
transported me   there are stages in each indiscretion and steps were taken   the
theater of her dance skirt opening all over Europe each with a seamstress backstage
stitching dancers to their steps   the past is a step that steps lightly into you its
steps are your breath its steps are the state you meant to return to taking the next
step   thread of the leash let go   there is a dropped stitch, no?   the token
smokes in its slot   have you begun a bag count, is there a sky to this loss? A force
a force a force and the war it hooked the end of the world on   its front door is the
look I saw on your face in the newspaper, sergeant   It unlocks me   title page of a
lost book in a library gone   the dog, your enemy, cover-up routine   icemaker,
deliver this to the bedside table   behind glass step lightly, it was liquid once
and will be again   the baby rattle of a bottle of suicide Tylenol   Lost Stitch
handmaiden, this is your talk show   there's room on the couch nothing to lose,
lost stitch, I recollect you from the cast   the dancer dancing death forever awake
his mourning body circling in   his costume like a bag cast all the way down the
body   first stitch, lost   at exhibition there was no foot upon the pedal of the
sewing machine.

McCormick's Reaper

Your credit's good, it isolates
the wheat, is strong enough
to push it toward the attachment blade
reciprocating to clear

the yield an acre gives ten men
to only five; halve them
where they stand again, halve them and
halve him, but an inkling

yielding where there was a man. Come
to the window, see for
yourself: Are you not in the house?
Are you not in bed hearing

yourself in the acre binding
shocks together with one
self-same stalk containing hundreds?
I rise, my guarantee.

I rise so you don't have to. Every
now and then a rattlesnake shimmies
into the shock and rises with me.

Eighty-blade Sportsman's Knife, by Joseph Rodgers & Sons

Do not think of the secret transvection of the
blade of the balisong counter-
rotating with such teleportal stealth
it arrives cold at the neck, a vampire knife
transforming in air from sheath
to edge and back again in a pulse like
the unaccountable translucent blades
of a helicopter;

even that tool is misnamed a "butterfly knife"—
underscoring an unfulfilled
wish for gradual metamorphosis,
and the two handles of the butterfly knife
only look like wings as if
hung on the thorax by Richard Serra—
no not hung, just propped against each other
temporarily; life

is improvisational, also death. All things
slip. But another name for the
butterfly knife I find more fitting is
"Manila Folder"; I'll take world capitals
for two hundred plus ancient
technology (at least as old as the
Roman Empire) by which a blade pivots
into its own hilt. It

sounds like a place to file old receipts, Manila
Folder, but it only files one
blade over and over. It is not grace
or contempt, but repetition that sharpens
me, and as repeating your
own name contaminates it the same way
a human's touch repels a mother bird
from her eggs, I don't think

I want to think about me today or ever.
Ever received mail intended
for another? The eighty-blade sportsman's
knife is that archive. Look yourself up in cross-
referenced alternative lives.
The one-fact file of the butterfly knife
burns obsolescent like the pathetic
bioluminescence

of a dead firefly I might as well have stepped on
last night on my own kitchen floor,
while the body of my sportsman's knife, as
abiding as the roach into whose august
DNA a whole volume
of the *New York Times* was proposed to be
spliced, throbs in a flash of holy fire that
refines this Library

of Congress instead of engulfing it. I once
mailed myself my sportsman's knife in
a box sealed so tight I could not open
it without what was inside and my heart flipped
the various blades open

in silence inside the closed box. What vault,
what depository. What catalog
of hot tools. Splayed it is

a bouquet of all the ways a point mutates. It
contains the bayonets piercing
the chain mail at the end of the mind. Screw
driver. Bottle opener. Isolation
wire cutter. The room goes dark.
Coupling for corkscrew; multi-purpose hook;
hard wire cutter and harder wire cutter;
reamer; flesh hook; release

the awl. I do not believe in awe. Every pick
has a lock it alone fits. I
do not believe even one screw ever
was stripped. It is a joy to place the Philips-
head in the Philips-shaped slits
in the world. Twisting it, you can feel the
rotation of the earth, you can feel the
revolution in your

wrist. You've seen psychopaths arranging implements;
resist the primitive urge to
adapt your tools. Suspect what's makeshift; this
era is task-specific. When we use the
tool intended for the job
we are neutral. The right tool for the right
task is objective truth.

Iron Door Knocker the Shape of a Man's Face, by Feetham

Has no fly laid a sac of eggs
in the wet hole in the house finch
dead on the back porch
a week, ten days, not even
the eyes missing, sometimes
I sit by it and read, it's March,
there is fatness to the air, walking
to the bus, back from the bus, I
miss the confidence
swift burial of the dead
gives us. I used to believe the wild
takes care of itself. I used to believe
maggots arise
like a spring of death
that need only be tapped,
but the flow of incarnation
is much too slow and nothing
comes to debride the flesh
so that my finch
can matriculate into the hall
of its next house
the door of which
is guarded.
You've seen door knockers
with the faces of men. In the novel,
the face warms to your approach,

but it's so few of us who can even
get our body all the way through
the cold negative space
of an unstrung tennis racket
we're holding. Pilloried in a past life,
who joins us here in this awful heat
clinging to the screen
door? A swarm of mayflies clutching
the wire mesh on their only night on earth.
They defile it until they
die, though it's not exactly
true they live their whole
lives in one humid day.
They were larvae first, that takes years,
then they emerge starving with no
mouth. Someone hates us very
much. If you walk back from
the lake late in the afternoon, as my
mother did when a girl, you'll find thousands
on the kitchen door when you return. A thousand
bodies who want in. I don't
want there to be a thousand faces
on the other side but
my grandmother must have seen them
when she pushed open the door for you.

Project Huia

for my fifth wedding anniversary

White-tipped huia feather, are you afraid
    of the parallel world where notes are penned
        on the black vellum of black lambs in white ink
        with the feathery end of the feather

instead of the shaft of the quill,
    as in negatives of the film we used to use
        that told suffused narratives of our burning
        antipodean bodies handed over

the precipice of the Rite Aid counter
    in an envelope within an envelope that proved
        the soul is filed in the body neatly but variously
        in strips the size

of bookmarks indicating where to come back to?
    There were bright redundant birthday
        parties and a trip to the Lincoln Memorial
        where, ghost children, my sister and I

placed translucent hands on Lincoln's obsidian knees;
    glancing off the Vietnam Veterans milky
        Memorial Wall, our faces pooled
        into the survivors' names and,

much later, visiting the other arctic house in Central Park,
    penguins with reverse markings
        sliding recklessly across black ice
        make the afterlife seem as dangerous

as this one and I wonder if I die
in the other world, will I rematerialize, as I
recall the white, white alligator, whom my father caught
in pictures

—the negatives of which neutralize the image—
rising from the Mississippi behind the New Orleans
aquarium like the emissaries from hell that
breach the gate

in horror movies?
Some believe unfastening the feather box containing one huia tail
feather laid there ceremonially not long before
announced extinct

unseals a box beyond containing a huia
missing a tail feather but poised otherwise to return to the earth,
and opening the feather box
in your uncle's

kitchen, indeed the adjustment of the world's cabin pressure
that results when the lid of a sarcophagus
in the parallel world, exhaling
in the manner of the

mouth of a mason jar like a bantam valve, raises
a sigh from my lungs. You've heard of the Butterfly Effect,
by which the still wings
of a butterfly in Newark, New Jersey

hasten the death by exposure of a girl in Cook Strait;
this is the Law of the Pressure Chamber:

stale air escaping an opening crypt
inhaled converts into divine

inspiration. Built on the site of a massive earthquake
in the Hawkes Bay region of New Zealand,
where the high school boys behind the huia cloning scheme
grew up heirs of

ancestors browsing in either the fine department store
or public library when the brick buildings
sifted into the opening earth
as if panned for gold over an

abyss and none was found, an Art Deco city
with lightning bolts and sun bursts carved
into its white stone walls stylizes
annihilation. Obliteration is an

opportunity. I was thinking this the other day
over cocktails at the Palmer House in downtown
Chicago; designed after the Great Fire,
the ceiling of its

barbershop was tiled with silver dollars
that flash inwardly when customers close their eyes
like the first symptoms of the kind of migraine
that makes you pull onto the shoulder

of the road and put your head down on the steering wheel.
How will I proceed? With a sixpence coin
in her wedding shoe a bride presses on in prosperity,
but it unnerves

me to face the New Zealand sixpence
        with its depiction of the female huia
                long extinct when minted by the coinage committee;
            and naming a high school mascot

huia even ever after
        casts hopelessness over the team.
                No matter who wins or loses, the huia's absence
            at rugby matches suggests that doom befalls

us all. The scrum at the center of the world
        has no ball in it, which is why the high school boys
            perform the infinitesimal operation
            to clone the huia

in which one of them holds down the warm magpie
        that alighted on the sill of their locker room
                while another inserts one cell of a huia
                tail feather obtained from

a ceremonial huia feather box
        into its magpie ovum. The surgery is so minute
            it's more like the uncanny wish that kills
            a man clipping the

feather affixed with a single stitch
        from the band of the Duke of York's trendsetting
            huia-feathered hat. It might sound
                overly dramatic when I tell you the magpie

teeters a little under the weight of the cell
        on its way to perch before the wavy mirror in its new cage,

but remember it's smaller than you, and
though a fraction

of a fraction of what's measurable in your hand,
in proportion to a magpie,
the weight of the huia cell
is the *World Book Encyclopedia*, Volume 8:

the huia's habitat; the hunt; the king's hat;
his hapu; Hamlet, referring to a performance
or event taking place without its central
figure, the HMS

Endeavor; the hatchet; a half-breed; and speaking
of Hollywood, remember that scene in *Rosemary's*
Baby when Mia Farrow sees her warped reflection
in a toaster

while she devours raw meat? I wonder
how the magpie will stand to look at herself,
even strong as she once was lifting a packet
of Sweet'N Low right off the breakfast

table on the first morning after my wedding and flying it
clear out the window to a part
of the island off limits to me; and don't they build nests
of barbed wire, one

of which encloses three stranded, rotting eggs right now
in a ring of concertina while near by
in the high yellow grass a possum with its throat cut
confounds a gardener?

The high school boys know best though,
        desperate to feel the soft breast of the huia again,
           and hear the song written
                on the label of the huia diorama at the

National Museum: *huia,*
        easy to remember. I'm singing it now
           to the mouse with the ear on its back;
              I'm singing it to the Tasmanian tiger who

was called back. The brink rocked in its wake. And don't
        mistake its dog face and the marsupial
           pouch on its striped midsection
              for a mutation as quaint as a flip book of wild-

life juxtapositions. The same force that arranged it the first time
        also dropped a struck tree on the last bucardo on Earth.
           The last of something
              drains every day. Watch it go.

I don't love you anymore. I love you. I don't
        love you anymore. Who can trust a daisy
           with regenerating petals? That my car keeps on going
              with my foot off

the pedal makes me suspect a perpetual wrist watch,
        a Rolex Submarital Oyster, but still,
           I like my death proud. What strikes
              me about the isle of flightless birds is

how unloved I am except on Earth. Let the lights
        down the exit aisle blaze like the glowworm

when it hunts. And wouldn't it be something
              if bioluminescence was a magic

lantern that projects digestion on cave walls.
              The green light intensifies
                            and the show starts. Picture Daisy's iridescent dock, then
                            the slow enzymatic process of the

assimilation of the captive mayfly into light itself.
              If you leave your scarf on the cave floor
                            it will raise a shadow of mold before
                            the third act—but I'm trying

to stay focused on the real world where your own suit
              hanging in the dark closet throughout
                            the rainy season grew a fine mold, a dusting—enough
                            snow to close a road in this

wet, temperate country where Cook's men took
              glowworms for fairy folk and if only the small, imported
                            white mice had already crossbred with fluorescent
                            jellyfish they would have

twinkled down the exit plank
              in every sack of whatever it was men traded for sex around here,
                            where the silver fern shoots what looks and feels
                            like a monkey arm from its

dank heart and the sailors might as well have just swum
              across to find their love—the genetic material of
                            the silver fern does, crossing an ocean
                            on the verso of

each frond; when I pressed one in a book overnight
        it left a goldleaf outline chalked where the body was
            when I untucked it in the morning;
                gold dust; ash of a newspaper

ad; slag of a ticket stub; quiet as embers of a love note
        or the cremated cell of a huia that failed.
            What is the proper hostess gift?
            Magpies like bright things

and so do I. I'm going on a picnic
        and bringing Ben Franklin's key. The cold sun
            firing off its teeth distracts me so, I forget where I'm going.
            Did I lie down in

the snow? It's a bit cold here in winter
        which is summer in the rest of the world
            and a horizontal rain makes me feel like the planet is spinning
            off to the left or

that I am walking sideways—
        another 90 degrees and the mappa mundi–illuminated species
            walking on hands will have predicted
                how I creep head down, view

to the faultline, which has the counter intentions
        of the horizon, is always the dangerous line
            just crossed. I can feel the wind
                from the opposite pole blow through cracks in

the porch. I can smell the roots of everything.
        The world watches, but I wonder how this must

look through the keyhole? The shimmer of wet
          leaves is the spotting vision of something

much bigger than me in pain.
     A light goes on and off in the margin.
          Lie down in the blind spot with me and there's nothing
               we can't do. St. Augustine didn't see how the offspring

of a single host could have reached
     the Antipodes—thus it must be clean
          of life. But how easy to drip
               right through the thirst of the earth and trickle out the other side a

layer of ice on the twisting highway.
     I am mostly water, anyway,
          albeit corrosive, or so I gather from the effect
               a trapper's body had on the

meat dangled into his shotgun wound,
     which I read about as a child.
          Shot through the stomach, alive, he was a living window
               an army surgeon gazed into. Drawing the

line up every few hours,
     the surgeon charted the slow decomposition
          of beef lowered like bait into the gape.
               When ice fishing where fish are starving or tossing coins in

an acid fountain, I cannot withdraw my offer.

Dear Ralph Lauren,

Might I, if there's one in stock, be sent the
Ralph Lauren Winchester Tote
shaped like the feedbags I've seen strapped on the
fierce muzzles of the horses in pictures
children are shown to depict
for them how tasks, such as the
feeding of horses, were accomplished in
the Old West. As you
know, the weave of the wool
of the Winchester Tote

is gun-check plaid, so please don't confuse my
order with permission to
perform the background check you would need were
you selling me a gun, Ralph Lauren, or
with the booth where I would check
mine as I would, say, my coat,
entering a restaurant. No, I would
not relinquish it,
as some would prefer to
hold their fur in their lap

as they dine than leave it in strangers' hands
and what's more, you may not look
into my past, Ralph Lauren, and I will
not look into yours, though I note that the
plaid known as gun-check consists
of infinite weaved stairways
leading up and up and up and atop
not even one small
refined wool landing stands
a screener who would stop

either of us from climbing. Isn't this
the tartan of our clan, Ralph
Lauren? In a picture, I saw your dog,
Rugby, seated in the passenger seat
of your Jaguar and I dream
I'm holding him on my lap
as we're waived through the unmanned tollbooths of
the Jersey Turnpike.
You know the system; we
need not pay until we

exit. Do you mind if I call you Dad?
You can call me Little Sure
Shot, as Sioux Chief Sitting Bull called Annie
Oakley when he adopted her. And here's
something else called "Annie," Dad:
a complimentary train
ticket with a hole prepunched through the list
of destinations
is named "Annie" for the
tiny holes she shot through

the decks of playing cards that Buffalo
Bill dealt one by one into
the dusty air and I wonder if the
Turnpike ticket in the glove compartment
is likewise preclocked. Does it
make you sad to know Annie
Oakley was not Annie Oakley's real name?
Where do we stand when
pseudonyms take nicknames,
like my real father, for

instance, who was born Abraham and called
Dad my whole life and Hank by
my mother, was named for the forefather
Abram whose name was changed by God, whose real
name may never be uttered,
as yours may not be, but how
safely written here in the ghetto of
these parentheses
(Lifshitz). (Polo by Ralph
Lifshitz.) Often I wake

from this dream quoting an apocryphal
Bible chapter where Adam
brands the animals. At home in the Ralph
Lauren Home Collection the walls of my
childhood bedroom are painted
Winchester Gray for my real
father's unloaded shotgun that stood for
him in the guestroom
closet. I'm already
riding shotgun with it

with Rugby asleep on my lap in your
silver Porsche 550
Spyder, designed by the first son of the
designer of Hitler's Volkswagon, so
you might as well adopt me.
The top's down and as the wolf
lowers into the Spyder, the spider
enters the vein, vain
enters glory and I
enter the country club

with you through the glory hole that is the
hidden opening through which
that unseen ball the Polo Player on
your logo is always chasing always
just rolled. Furious divots
stipple the polo grounds and
I feared the forward waving his mallet
like a tomahawk
until you told me the
logo is based on me

merely hailing a cab. Why, Dad, do you
translate me so tormented,
so raving, driving my muddy pony
with death spurs and blood on my stick. This is
a brutal way to sell shirts.
I've never seen a button-
down as beautiful as the one you lost.
I remember when
you lowered it to half-
mast on Labor Day, but

every day is Labor Day and the shop
(don't make me say your heart) is
open, open, open. The wind flogging
the white flag of your flapping shirt makes it
appear to have a man in it.

Multi-purpose Steamship Furniture, by Taylor & Sons

is made of patent cork fiber for buoyancy, a room
within a room, life-couch docked confidently in a suite
in which everything else would sink or dissolve into a crypt room
many leagues below, roomy
enough to allow a whole school of mackerel and their natural enemy, the shark, to
    change
direction through catacombs of mouldering china sunk from table settings in
    ballrooms, dinner rooms, tea rooms, and the private bedrooms
of independent travelers of independent means into craggy heaps like the cliff faces
    on which manor houses fall to ruin, indistinguishable—from the distant
    view of a traveler spending
the final twists of journey dwelling in awe on it—from the land itself. In dwelling,
    she both must spend
time contemplating and inhabiting the gloomy walks, the compromised stairs
    opening on room after room
as her life
depends on it, while she in possession of Multi-purpose life-

affirming Steamship Furniture floats from her comparable devastation lively
in the manner she reposed upon it, reading, I suppose, as the first order of
    multi-purposefulness is conversion from couch to bed, sitting room to bedroom
as the whole doubles as life
raft, as life
preserver. Life itself doubles in the face of water. Put a stick in it, you know what I
    mean. Refraction is the one sweet
clue to suggest going back in time, but a moment, or is it forward? you would keep
    your integrity as you plunge into water, but, as it is, life's
series of steppings forward sift short-lived
as through prisms, ever-changing,
as graceful or abrupt as a change
in conversation, depending who's talking. Sometimes life

depends upon the ease of such digressions, and the energy spent
planning to slip undetected into recesses darker yet, whole nights spent

considering the most likely architecture between two known doors on unlikely ends
    of unexplored ruin, balances with that spent
finally traveling it, but a moment, a spark's life.
Put your hand in water. You divide between two rooms, this and the one light
    hesitates to pass through the border of in which you spend
the afternoon beside yourself, an alternative taking place unperceivably later. Even
    in a lifetime spent
going in and out of water, the lost time doesn't amount to much—it won't add up to
    a few more minutes in the bedroom
with you on a rainy November morning, which is what I'd spend
my border change on were reimbursements made for time lost being refracted and
    refracted almost every time we move through this slow, cheating universe that
    spends
me even as I step closer to you. Let us remember to move between realms indivisibly
    in darkness, as Multi-purpose Steamship Furniture, by Taylor & Sons converts
    swiftly and sweetly
without a light to read by from cabin furniture to life preserver before the wave
    rising beneath the very suite
it occupies fully spends
the force of its crest, which is to say, it changes
unchanged.

Change
not given. Everything valued diminishes. Spent
the whole day reading again, and by the end, had to change
my opinion of what I'd hoped were ghosts changing
the living,

but they changed
suddenly material as if winter passed over the novel and everything numinous
    froze in a quick change
in the weather of mystery. The room
emptied, the room
key turned silently, and the change
in me was complete. Sweet,
sweet

Taylor & Sons, is this any way to save oneself? Opportunist, another name for
    multi-purpose, questions the eponymous sweetness
of the rose, for which I name this changing
stanza "my sweet
one." How will I use the word sweet
again? How will I spend
my light? How will I use the word sweet?
How will I use the word sweet?
How does my life
differ from my life?
How will I use the word sweet?
There is no room
in this life, no life in this room.

Lustron: The House America Has Been Waiting For

Room for all our sons. Time
saver. Put away your hammer. Four
rooms with the last
room on the left facing the side yard for which an extension is already planned. Times
change, so should your house. Tomorrow is prefabricated. It's coming on the bed of
    a truck. It has a living
room in another dimension, an opening in the crowded continuum with
room for overnight guests. Some of them won't want to come. They won't be
    missed. A vigilante highwayman is pulling onto the exit ramp. He
spent his last quarter at the tollbooth at the end of the past. The future is coming. It
spends its time, the new money, on golf courses and gardening. It has four
rooms and an eat-in kitchen. It's a straight shot here and when your new
life pulls up it will resemble a train car that jumped the tracks to avoid the heroine
    who's been tied there her whole
life and now has a chance to

live in a house with four
rooms and a sun porch. Its name is Lustron: luster on steel, the luster is porcelain.
    The future
lives in a porcelain-reinforced four-room house with a doily under every vase like
    the clean white shadow grace would cast were it not the source of light itself.
    It's so safe here, porcelain flowers
live forever in a porcelain-reinforced
saferoom, luster on steel like
living in the barrel of a mythic Glock. Imagine a whole
life that feels like the satisfaction of passing through security with undetectable
    weaponry in your carry-on. The future is in the overhead compartment and it
    won't be long until it's safe to turn it on. It
changes a man to know it's near. I left some
change in the giant putty-colored bed pan into which I emptied my

life; why don't you get yourself some gum to chew while you gossip about my past in
     the airport lounge unless you've already
spent so much backyard dynamite preparing your lot for your new house that you're
     wading in the curls of
spent firecracker wrappers contemplating the boundless footfalls you

spent mounting the backstairs of Victorian
life while the future parked around the corner was ready to pull up to your curb and
     deliver the dreams you earned on the battlefield where you
spent your body. I think you heard the engine idle and thought it was your
     neighbor's television's poltergeist
spending its broadband on satellite coverage of a black hole pulling nothing. I've
     heard the control
room monitors broadcasting the activity of every grave and it breaks my heart to
     learn Mrs. Winchester and I were both wrong about eternal revenge. Not one
     soul has ever returned—they all go forward with their anger to
spend deep in the future. In fact, they
save it up, adjust for inflation, and always back both sides comparably in the name
     of perpetuation. Lustron has a no-nonsense Westchester model house, which
     I like to think of as a Winchester Mystery House for a Western Destiny already
     won. See how fast the past slips into the future; it's a matter of a few letters and
     a notary public to change your
spent cartridge and you're ready to aim again. It
changes a man to start over. It
changes his perspective—but it doesn't
change the future, the future is a prefabricated four-room house with nowhere to
     run. This is what I mean when I tell you to
spend the day reading in bed, maybe

spend some time in the tub, or watch a made-for-television movie. You can't change your

life so why not enjoy it safe in the knowledge you already live in the porcelain-
enameled mythical Glock everyone's always talking about smuggling into the
cockpit.

Change seemed to be in the air when the privacy curtain dividing cockpit from cabin

changed to a locked door, but Glock first manufactured plastic curtain rods, and the
future was always sliding open in its name. It slips into the shower with you, and
though radio-sheer, you sensed it pulsing near the radio-opaque cuticle scissors
you exchanged for your ticket at the last security check. The past is a hangar of
manicure scissors at Newark International Airport; the future grows claws.

Rumor has it the future stationed air marshals at Denny's to listen for certain words
to be spoken, like the pool of monkeys forced to type until the name of God
appears, and once uttered a sting like a rapture will be triggered. The word is
Lustron. Luster on steel. Four

rooms and a bomb shelter. A porcelain in- and exterior. Let the chosen disappear
and stay a few more minutes here on Earth with me. The museums are empty
and free and I want to run my hand along the underside of the porcelain
patroness Madame Pompadour's desk to find the hidden drawer where she kept
her Glock. She

changed her will and left it to us. Imagine a house so poised you can live in its
teacups. Four rooms and a creamer. They survive revolutions. Some of them are
virgins. The future is a Louis XVI teacup

saving itself for you. The tea is Paul Ceylon, popular with those who sometimes
orders take and sometimes afternoon tea with something savory to tide them
over until probate passes. The Pope sanctioned it and the future

saved you a seat at the Lustron corporate anniversary party. The cake is a simple
    one-level sheet shaped like a Lustron House, which is to say, the cardboard box
    a mythical Glock shipped in. Through transubstantiation it tastes like blood.
    Everything
changes
save the Glock.
Save a piece in your freezer; it's the wedding cake for your commitment to the future.
    Four rooms and a bride who
spends everything but
saves box tops to redeem a year later for what she gave up. Throw things to the river,
    but
save the Glock; you can take it with you.
Life is a series of exchanges; everything valued escalates; the luster is porcelain, even in
    the next
life. Trade is the mother of beauty. Heaven will be knowing no one can
save up. There are four
rooms in eternal salvation. Four
rooms and a motherless Glock.

Silverware, by J. A. Henckels

Even though the fashion of courtesans
to use a tiny fork to eat sticky dishes
that would otherwise stain their fingers
prompted a church ban on this utensil
with which the devil himself prods
whores into the fire and might explain the omission
of a fork at some place settings to attend to
the delicacies flowing into the wedding
banquet in the Final Panel of Botticelli's
painting of Boccaccio's pale moral tale
regarding the eternal hunt of a fleeing ghost
Maiden by two ghost dogs
and a ghost Knight who freshly slays her
every Friday and feeds her heart to his dogs,
I fear the omission foreshadows what I
discovered missing this morning in an inventory
of my silverware drawer: two forks from my
wedding registry, smooth silver of spare design
featureless save a single line
where the fork head meets its body,
which we chose ten minutes before Macy's closing
and gone now for who knows how long,
or whether in a pair of incidents or if in tandem,
certainly here in my own home, as I never
bring my silverware out with me as early
nobility did in red velvet-lined cases
like medical bags whose portability
brought the invention of the fork slowly
to dinner parties all across Europe
and into France finally when a Marchese
Pucci in the court of Catherine
de Medici—a son of that same family

who commissioned the Botticelli wedding
painting which hasn't enough forks and
makes me so sorry, like a bad wife who
loses everything—lifted a fork to his lips
at a court feast where all other guests
ripped the joint with their teeth.
Looking at silverware cases with recesses
the shape of missing forks makes me wonder
what else is missing.
Space left free for forms so long gone makes me
suspicious of this world and the stillness
of its materials that refuse
to meld together in the wake of absence
and I long to relinquish what remains
of my forks to the forge in Solingen, Germany, where
Johannes Henckels registered his trademark
twin symbol with the Cutlers' Guild in 1731
and began immediately planning my wedding silver
only for it to be disposed of with the cake box
or undervalued, as Montaigne writes: "I could dine without a
tablecloth, but to dine in the German
fashion, without a clean napkin, I should
find very uncomfortable as I
make very little use of either spoon
or fork," though he did likely make use
of the point of his knife to lift meat off a common plate
and since fingerprints in the salt are a sign
of a thief, to dip into the saltcellar,
before which he would first have used a slice
of bread to wipe any spit off the knife
that may have accumulated there
if he was one of those whom Richelieu

wished to criticize in his promotion
of a new knife formed without the point
one picked one's teeth at table with
before Louis XIV finally ordered
all remaining knifepoints ground off because
is dinner where we settle arguments?
even if the handles of early cutlery
resemble the handles of pistols
big enough to collapse the business ends into
for safer transport to table, and hiding
as Richelieu says, "in lines written
by the most honest man, I will
find something to hang him?"
Behind each silver flower Henckels hammers
in each viney handle there is an arrow
that points to me. Let me be
as streamlined as my knife when I say this.
As cold as my three-pronged fork that
cools the meat even as it steadies it.
A pettiness in me was honed
in this cutlers' town, later bombed,
in which Adolf Eichmann, who was born there
alongside my wedding pattern, could hear
the constant sharpening of knives
like some children hear the corn in their hometowns
talking to them through the wind.
The horizon is just the score they breathe through
like a box of chickens
breathing through a slit.
My pettiness counts the knives again.
It holds out a cutting board
when you come home with bread.

I have been under the impression
knives grow sharp through use.
By making knives we make
all making possible. The face
of my serving spoon is slotted
in the shape of an ancient footstep
of an undiscovered extinct relation
of our hummingbird
who let his frantic sole
be traced only once in private.
I am very small without you.
I am mailed into the incision.
Walking toward you
I return my remaining
silver in order to forget
the interstellar swoosh of you
sharpening the knife before carving a turkey
we have two less forks to pick at with.
O Horizon, infinite poem
of creation's silence.
Friends, I only serve six of you now
that two of my forks are gone.

H5N1

My mask aches, and a drowsy numbness pains
my lungs, as though the inhale/exhale valve
I tightened to filter the avian strain
excludes bacteria blood needs to have;
is not want of resistance, but having
been too resistant in the past that slackens
me, while bacteria shape-shift on the tip
of the pen I put in my mouth after sharing
with you, my love, and though I know I lack
evidence, I taste superbug on my lips.

O for a capsule of Tamiflu sealed
in a crate in a warehouse in New Jersey leased
by Hoffmann-La Roche Inc. to make me feel
safe. I once stroked a figurine of a beast,
both man and bird, in the Roche (no connection)-
Dinkeloo refurbished wing of Egyptian
art at the Met and touched off an alarm
that sounded like a truck backing up through
the ages, a programmed bleat with which I'm
not saying not to touch me, but don't touch

me if you've lately played with something not
long dead even though when you admitted
you'd also have tossed a dead hen, warm with rot,
at your sister given the chance that the Turkish
twins confirmed dead of bird flu had to terrorize
each other, I agreed any of us would.
And who would not kiss the head of a swan
just to try to memorize
the softness of something wild? I should,
and I did, and I call upon and call upon

that kiss even as German pathologists
mount specimens of that swan's dissected heart. ·
Away! Away! I am grist
dabbed on the slide with you. They try to part
my cells from yours but I am airborne. The night
mists with fever and low, undetected
pathogenic virulence ruffles every
thrush's plumes. Let our path of contagious flight
take our infected bird's-eye view over
Merck World Headquarters. Maybe my vision warps,

but in the diseased light the building looks
to me like the Pentagon and flying toward it
my perspective matches the one from the
cockpit window of the hijacked jet
if fever can be said to concentrate
all the heavenly glare that must have bounced
off the cars parked in the secure lot at
9:43 AM,
for here there is no light, save from the warehouse
loading dock where an unmarked freight

truck slowly reverses. This is where
to enter the warehouse at the center
of night where dawn's combustible stockpile
is stacked in neat boxes that tempt me to pry
their lids all at once like the flaps of an advent
calendar whose days flare simultaneously
when I flip them open to reveal that while
I am living I am dead in another
part of the same building. Maybe this is
why I feel nothing. The something dead you touched,

was it my hair? But here there's antidote
enough to sustain us forever.
The malady only needs a box cutter
and we can administer the doses to each other
in the warehouse dark. A box cutter and
a glass of water; a box cutter, the other
knife we hold between us as we renew
our vows. The groom's cake is packing tape.
The bride's cake is Styrofoam. My blood
is something blue before I cough it up.

On the Abduction of Calvin Klein's Daughter Marci: A Captor's Narrative

Eternity, Escape, and Obsession fly the same neutral flag
in three shades of overcast steel. I was raised under it
in an orphanage with Brooke Shields and Kate Moss,
but everyone's my Daddy,
and we could hear the wind yawn through our birth
certificates. I was always one step behind,
an expendable caddy, while Kate carried the
burden of marking the nuance
where gray and grey collide

over the Atlantic and Brooke dated the Jordanian Prince.
We were ambassadresses from childhood, paid to live with
you like Jane Eyre and Pip. I remember Brooke
telling me reading is to
the mind what Calvins are to the body;
I took her hand in mine, and we went out of the
ruined place; and, as the evening mists had risen
long ago when I first left the
forge, so the morning mists

were rising now, and in the shadow of the uptown bus Calvin
Klein's daughter steps into the vestibule of her highrise.
The press suspected you of staging your own
daughter's kidnapping as a
publicity stunt, but after all these
years, I'm too exhausted to keep accusing you.
That morning on her way to school, Kate, Brooke, and I
convinced Marci to come with us
by telling her you were

about to die. In those days bus tokens had a bull's-eye at their
center; I remember focusing on the two bull's-eyes
in my fifth pocket all morning—one for me
and one for Marci—; you have
to be very small, much smaller than me,
to really use a coin pocket so Kate used to
make a game of placing things deep in ours that Brooke
and I could never retrieve. Kate
was the kind of baby

babies call out baby to from passing baby carriages. What's
cut even too wee for children's hands was cut for hers. Brooke
was the mastermind; when she darkened her smile
Kate knew to draw the tokens
from the portal to a smaller world that
was my pocket and now it was time to think hard
about what would make us weep as we boarded the
city bus with Marci. I don't
have to tell you Kate wept

for the fawns of hell and Brooke for the bucks of earth, but me, I touched
Marci's cold silk dress, and though I told Brooke and Kate I wept
for the worm, I really wept for the death I
came there to report. Your flag-
ship has a concrete floor austere as the
cellar we slept in before we were reborn. When
I can't remember the name of my own parent
company, I ask: You know what
comes between me and my

John Calvins? Nothing, except Judaism—and then I recall
the name of the corporation is Puritan. I can
still feel the feel of Marci's throat. I feel left
out sometimes when everyone's
quoting Traherne and Donne. I feel the bleat
vibrate my knife right through the goat. We live it to
the hilt, this life, and then we want still more on the
other side. I used to put a
pillowcase over my

head and haunt the ward just by passing down the aisle between the beds.
Brooke wrote the ransom note in lowercase Futura font
and signed it ckone. She whistled Oh my
darlin' Oh my darlin' Oh
into the heavy black telephone. It
took all Kate's strength to hold the receiver up. Brooke
was the mouth, but I was the ear. I still hear a
rush of water between all the
words I speak. Clementine

was the drowned eldest daughter of a 49er. She slipped right
into the American River. By the time the song
is over, her little sister is married
to the man Clementine loved,
but Kate, Brooke, and I never competed
for your hand. My dress slip is named for her and I
wear it when I want to slip into my childhood
to salvage something Kate slipped long
ago into my hip

pocket. What do I carry I outgrew the will to touch? Kate, Brooke,
and I never competed for this land, but it's ours as
much as anyone's. Bill Clinton said it was
wrong to manipulate us
children for commercial benefit; it
should not have been for profit. The nation is yet
very, very young and anything can happen;
I have Knicks courtside seats and great
expectations. I saw

you come staggering into the game, Calvin Klein, and there, into
the ear of Latrell Sprewell, heard you pardon us all for
our anger. I can feel the ball in my hands.
I can feel the boundaries
of the game come to pass.

Heroic Couplet

This is an

astral projection
disembodiment

left angular gyrus

When I came home last night I had my keys
but rang the bell so as to be received

by you

perceived location
actual location

Project Paperclip

"Project Paperclip" was the code name for the recruitment of Nazi
engineers of the V-2 Bomber into the American space program

Assembling prefabricated joinery
      of a botany lab in zero gravity
            two astronauts touching the same panel share a secret but
          let go with nothing

to conduct them words drip through eaves of rocketry,
      a first thaw rolling off a dagger of ice playing
          melismatic prisms off the radar that
            register and re-reg-

ister lapsing presences various
      as signals melting ice beam in evanescence,
          and one thing won't lead to next, no stairs
            to a landing where leaning from the railing

I could sail a love note folded
      into an airplane back into the front hallway in outer space
          where paper planes fail lift off
            and confessions scrawled in paper chassis fail

to retract, eternally lingering
      like lines of poems Chinese woodworkers once
          carved into joinery of portable furnishings
            to guide reassembly when the

maid charged with dismantling chairs
      in the rhododendron garden is called away
          before having time to reconstruct
            them in the fragrant orchard, leaving lines intended

to lead the front legs into the foreground
        of the seat unresolved—*The Universe is*—
             and—*Time is*—never to interlock
                with *Vast* and *Eternal*, as a famous guide-verse

reads, open on the wet grass
                (how will she join the pieces
                when Asian Longhorned Beetles
                colonize arm rails seatbacks
                headrests emendating what's
                written there by chewing a
                recess in the bamboo-strip

                veneer, a wall niche in a
                beetle cloister, laying eggs
                where a stone patron would a-
                wait the second coming deep
                in the alcove of the word),

        just dust, like words Chinese scholar Wan-Hoo
            carved in hinges of the chair he contructed
                to convey him to the moon before disintegrating

in moonlight. No log of the journey records this.
        No log of the journey exists.
            Just a powder. An ash. A dust so fine
                it's more a mist like the grain of a photograph

settling an integument on everything it touches.
        Grist of the material world while the immaterial
            grinds smaller yet—you've felt
                the filmy fog of ghosts—not

just the soul, but its words live on in the afterlife
       accessed in a game of anagrams
             with the dead every time we speak.
                    But why a detachable chair? Wouldn't something more

sturdy, unyielding at the hinge better bear one to the moon?
       Wan-Hoo told his wife,
             Alone on the moon won't it be convenient to carry
                my chair along on walks where there

will be no reference to lead me back to it
       and how hard the moon's ground appears from here, or
             alternatively, like a pond that seems a field
                when blooms of algae settle, though

my eyes indeed believe that they see a clearing
       of solid ground before them,
             the moon's prairie but a liquid
                I will need to convert my chair into a boat to float on.

             (When the maid returned many
             days later to reassem-
             ble the chairs and table, she
             found the pieces several
             ounces lighter, hollowed by
             Asian Longhorned larvae born

             voracious in the depths and
             now the table wobbles lunch
             of master and his guests be-
             cause the maid remembers how
             the assembly poem goes
             but it was full of exit

holes obscuring the letters
leading this front leg into
teeth cut to bite this hind leg
and this hind leg quavering
in a gape mouthing a dif-
ferent name.)

               (Perhaps memory is pre-
cise but when the room around
a favorite object changes
objects seem changed, too, or so
pilgrims concluded of the
coat racks in New England front

parlors that dropped the coats they
were built to suspend or worse,
the fainting couch further back
in the new house that fails to
soothe. "Memory Furniture"
is the name given colo-

nial furnishings built here
in America to seem
like those left behind but lack-
ing craftsmanship and the de-
tailed joinery of the one
in mind my new chair sways dan-

gerously she who seeks com-
fort here. Settling in it now,
yes, swaying.
Smoke rising from docu-
ments of experiments dis-
perses what's recorded through

the air. Burned letters bond so unintelligibly
        with one another in the spirit world of dead words that the
                periodic table assembled as
                    the burning reads,

in accordance with the art of phantom cabinetry,
        cobbles dark campaign furniture convertible
                for misremembering who gathers
                    there, signs what, how a box of

paperclips keeps sliding off a plane so unsteady in mind
        there's nowhere to place the teacup,
                the lid of which, by Chinese custom, the host
                    lifts only to signify to

his guest that his guest is dismissed.
        Get out—Get out—

                            the house whispers this. Have you
                            seen this movie? A simple
                            dream of a Victorian
                            house for nothing, a new fa-
                            ther for your children who chops
                            firewood in stacks neatly by

                            the kitchen door in piles where
                            if you look closely, you can
                            see Asian Longhorned Beetles
                            flashing through like shooting stars,
                            which indeed they are named for
                            in China—Starry Sky Bee-

tle—for white dappling on black
bodies. No one prays for you.
In Amityville, New York,
where this movie unfolds in
a house with two glass eyes that
blind a priest, where a call was

made but static chattered straight
from hell, Starry Sky Beetles
ate through I don't know how man-
y trees, having been acci-
dentally imported a-
sleep in the wood of shipping

crates unbeknownst, like gloss scrawled
in the margin enters text
when the hand of the scribe car-
ries it over, crossed from the
foreman's list onto the list
of nonindigenous pests

kept by the Department of
Agriculture. Alien
Species. Let me trace it: a
migratory path vivid
to the holy who see the
rails of fate like faint dashes

that mean *cut here* finally
crossing; there is a cata-
log in which the cross reference
loops but it calls the falcon

back to the wrong wrist and the
new bird suits—or worse, a nar-

rative something like canals
the otherwise relia-
ble Percival Lowell observed
through his telescope crisscross-
ing boiling sands of Venus?
Trade routes! Does it discredit

me if I picture gondo-
liering Venusians drifting
under low Venusian bridg-
es? You can pick most locks with
paperclips and likewise flood
canal locks of Venus with

a prick to the eye, for I
read in the *Science Times* re-
cently what Lowell took as wa-
terways were his own retinal
blood vessels writ on his own
vision—paths of seeing—. A

bridge, a city, a planet
deluged in blood with the pierce
of one paperclip bubbling
up from below, an inky
swell flooding the old cellar
of the house with all-seeing

glass eyes in Amityville.
I am unprepared for ghosts
—the weightlessness—a gateway
to hell, I can't sleep here an-
ymore—I am this house and
my glass eyes never close. Had

you lost an eye in World War
II you would have been fitted
with a glass ball made in a
marble factory in Lau-
scha, Germany, and seen the
new world from the point of view

of one globe knocked from orbit
in a game of marbles. Me-
nagerie of crystal balls
through which light passes, you have
a green tint of burning vol-
canic limestone quarried from

the green sand of Lauscha the
same as a queasy green au-
dience of glass forest an-
imals. (I don't lie. I make mistakes.
Worse, I lie to myself.) German glass tradi-
tion, so rich in examples
of "joke glass," from which one can

take drink in the shape of a
horn, a stag, a rabbit, a
bear, a pistol, a penis,
or a boot, was it from one

of these that Arthur Rudolph,
director of V-2 Rock-

etry at Dora, took Schnapps
with SS soldiers deep in
corridors where prisoners
of Buchenwald turned V-2
diagrams drawn by Von Braun
into the real thing?

Don't grow attached. Don't grow attached. Nothing lasts. I say this on
the day Tom Ford departs, but don't laugh; I began containing

Starry Sky Beetles in boxes of 42 syllables each
to honor my mother's birth in 1942,
three days after the B-29 Superfortress

flew
for the first
time (Japan was built of sticks),
but I say goodbye in 42 for each call Tom Ford fielded on
September 11, 2001 for the Yves Saint

Laurent purple peasant blouse.
The New York store wasn't open to the public yet
but in the back room 42 calls came through
for a silk peasant blouse that throws its purple

silk light back at the moon it came from, calls
which I shall account for backward in the manner
I count myself down to sleep: 42:
from a woman on the roof; 41:

from he who saw the first plane hit but boarded
  the subway anyway and sat in darkness
    with an inkling; from one
      without a plan; and one with the plan that will never work;

from the deck of the ferry, turned around, facing home;
  from the back of the room, a voice;
    from the envelope; it's the sea that shapes all things;
      from the foot of the bridge; 33:

for there is no water in the voice of the caller, I'm afraid I mean the moon's
  dust Sea of Tranquility;
    va banque; vacancy; vaccination;
    vacillation; vacuum;

the visionary; the vale; vagary; *Vanity Fair*;
  vampires; the vault; the volume;
    the video cassette; the view from Greenpoint;
      the vote; a vein in line at the blood bank

following around the corner; the vow;
  the viff; the vig; the veer; the veer again;
    the vulture; in the name of the V-2 Vengeance Bomber,
      which tolls silently, they toll for

thee; 9: let me describe to you a man
  I dreamed of as a child: there are two names
    for my beloved, one on this side of the world and one,
      alas, on the other, when it

breaks my heart to say them both,
        the heart calls twice; 7: from the cockpit; 6: from the fire;
                5: on the elevator, between floors stuck but with a signal;
                        how the receiver

hums on hold; there was a ghost
        before there was a body, it throws its voice,
                verbatim, drops an octave, verso, in the hallway; versatility;
                        the first call came from me.

Kuhl House Poets

David Micah Greenberg
Planned Solstice

John Isles
Ark

John Isles
Inverse Sky

Bin Ramke
Airs, Waters, Places

Bin Ramke
Matter

Michelle Robinson
The Life of a Hunter

Robyn Schiff
Revolver

Robyn Schiff
Worth

Rod Smith
Deed

Cole Swensen
The Book of a Hundred Hands